Horses and their World

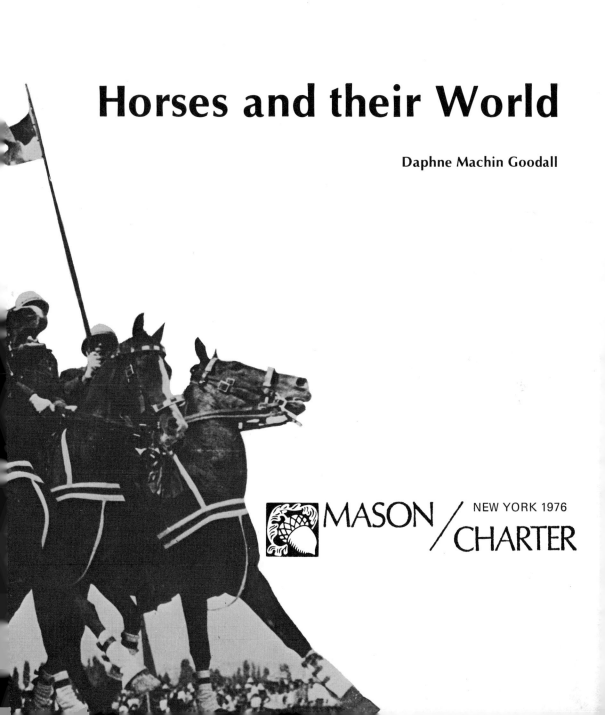

Horses and their World

Daphne Machin Goodall

MASON / CHARTER

NEW YORK 1976

Photographs without acknowledgement
are the copyright of the author.

First published in the
United States of America in 1976
by Mason/Charter Publishers, Inc.
641 Lexington Ave., New York City

Library of Congress Cataloging in Publication Data

Goodall, Daphne Machin.
  Horses and their world.

  1. Horses.   I. Title.
SF285.G63   636.1   76-14442
ISBN 0 88405 374 1

Printed in Great Britain

Contents

The Prayer of a Horse

To thee, Master, I offer my Prayer

Feed me, water and care for me, and when the day's work is done provide me with a shelter, a clean, dry bed and a stall wide enough for me to lie down in comfort.

Talk to me. Your voice often means as much to me as the reins. Pet me sometimes, that I may serve you more gladly and learn to love you.

Do not jerk the reins and do not whip me. Never strike, beat or kick me when I do not understand what you mean but give me a chance to understand you. Do not over-jump me and do not over-face me at fences which I cannot jump.

Watch me and if I fail to do your bidding see if something is wrong with my harness or feet.

Provide me with proper well fitting harness or saddlery and a comfortable bit, so that I may work well for you and in comfort.

Examine my teeth when I do not eat. I may have an ulcerated tooth and that can be very painful. Do not tie me up in an unnatural position, see that I am properly shod by a careful blacksmith, groom me often and keep me clean. Remember that I too, get tired after travelling in a horse-box for long distances.

And finally, Oh my Master, when my useful strength is gone, do not turn me out to starve or freeze, or sell me to be slowly tortured on a long journey to meet my end; but do thou, my Master, take my life in the kindest way, and thy God will reward thee here and hereafter. Do not consider me irreverent if I ask this in the name of He who was born in a stable.

(With slight variations from the original)

Introduction

This book is about the lives that horses lead in their own unique world. If, in the text, I have allowed myself to reminisce here and there, bringing in aspects of my own experience, it is because horses have always been a part of my world. Indeed from the time when, at the early age of three, I was scraped off a diminutive Shetland pony by the posts of a wicket gate and vowed vehemently that I would never ride a 'hunting horse' again, until the present day, my life has been involved with horses. I have been fortunate enough to discover horses in many countries of the world and, through the lens of my camera, catch them on film for posterity. In this way the Posener colts have been caught in their moment of happy abandon. Ponies, Thoroughbreds, jumpers, heavy horses, a cob and many others of different breeds have come and gone, with their lively temperaments, their individual likes and dislikes, their characteristic abilities—a vivid kaleidoscope of bays, greys, browns or chestnuts.

I am very happy to have had this chance to try to show readers the nature of horses and ponies as they go about their activities in their own private world. Although their world is largely dominated by the whims and egocentricities of man, we should not overlook the fact that horses have played, in the past, a leading rôle in man's own civilisation, even as they now play a leading rôle in his relaxation. Because they are essentially the only animals in the world to have shared physically man's competitive nature in sport and war, horses will perhaps succeed in turning this spirit away from self-destruction towards a happier destination amongst the pleasures of sport and nature.

'The state is governed from the back of a horse' runs an ancient Chinese saying. If only every politician realised too, that: 'Paradise on earth lies on the back of a horse' and learned just some of the disciplines required to become a true horseman or woman, then perhaps we would all be less governed and more governable. Indeed, it is not by accident that many of the best loved rulers, also perhaps some of the most ambitious in the world, have been closely involved with horses. Many have shown themselves too, to be horselovers and the horses with whom they shared their world were fortunate.

Is it too much to hope that readers will pause to reflect and will be able to assure themselves that the horses or ponies which add so much pleasure to their lives, are equally fortunate?

Daphne Machin Goodall
Henny, 1975

7

1 Wild and Free

It is approximately five thousand years since the horse was first domesticated to serve the purposes of man. We cannot be precisely certain and we could, perhaps, add on another two thousand years if one is convinced that the Cañaforas mural in eastern Spain, executed during the Mesolithic period, is a representation of real domesticated horses. It could well be that horses were domesticated by peoples of whom we have little or no knowledge historically even further in the distant past and at geographically distant places, and it is never advisable to insist that domestication took place for sure and beyond dispute at a certain fixed time (see my *A History of Horse Breeding*).

Wherever and whenever the first horse was tamed, it was most certainly the turning point in the life of the tribe or society which discovered the potential usefulness of its new-found friend. Domestication did not, of course, happen overnight, but was a gradual progression growing out of experience with domesticated reindeer, oxen and onager. Of primary importance was the chance element. A situation had to arise where a herd of wild horses happened to inhabit the region of a tribe which was beginning to experiment with the domestication of other animals. Another hindrance to progress must have been that by comparison with the domesticated animals already named, wild horses disappearing on a distant horizon in a cloud of dust at the sight or sound of man would not appear to be of much use to an immobile society or indicate a progressive future. It is possible to live in a region, with a person or with an object for a very long time without realising its potential.

The nomadic tribes seem to have been the first to have found a use for the wild, primitive horses in their locality. Grazing herds had to be moved to seasonal grazing grounds. In central Asia, camel and oxen were used for pack and draught transport, so why not a captured pony? It was then but a short step to place a person upon its back instead of the pack. The fifty centuries that have since elapsed have seen, on the one hand, quite enormous strides, not only in the domestication of the horse but in its civilising influence on man. However, on the other hand, its position amongst nomadic tribes has remained almost static, with the exception perhaps, of an effort towards slightly improved selective breeding.

In the Forest of Popielno, in the former province of East Prussia, now under the direction of the Polish State Studs, there is a domesticated herd and two completely wild herds of Forest Tarpan (see Plate 1). Studies of these groups have provided much valuable information about the toughness and hardiness of these wild primitive horses, for instance, they never abort nor do they catch cold.

Many breeds of domestic horses and ponies in Europe and in Asia, like the Achal Teké (see Plate 2) owe their descent to the prehistoric Tarpan. And the Tarpan itself, regenerated from primitive stock, once roamed in wild herds throughout Europe as far as the Ural Mountains. Achal Teké horses are herded in *tabuns* on the steppes and plains of Turkmene as they have been for many centuries, like the Kirghiz ponies. The former are noted for their phenomenal memories and sense of direction as well as for their endurance and stamina. Since the nomad often had to ride far and fast, some Achal Teké horses have taken part successfully in long-distance tests over many hundreds of miles.

The immediate ancestor of the Achal Teké, the Turkmene horse, also provided foundation blood for the Thoroughbred race-horse which, during the past three centuries, has proved itself to be one of the world's superior breeds. Many breeders of horses tirelessly strive to produce better animals by careful selection, but some members of the human race bring about a marked degeneration by their lack of discrimination.

The legend of the Heavenly horses is well known but it has a simple explanation (see my *A History of Horse Breeding*). Translated, the word *Tien Shan* means Celestial Mountains, and it was from this that the legend of the Heavenly horses arose. The Celestial Mountain horses were so called by the Chinese, whose Emperor Wu-ti sent envoys 3,000 miles to try to obtain them. Celestial Mountains has exactly the same meaning as when we talk of the Welsh Mountains with reference to Welsh Mountain ponies. Legend has it that mares running on these vast grass plains were covered by the winds of heaven, and there is also very little doubt that wild stallions were also at large and were perfectly capable of assisting the winds! History has shown that these stallions were an improved type of those used by the far-off Chinese of the same era.

In the distant Altai range of mountains, many hundreds of miles to the north of the Tien Shan, the Asiatic wild horse is trying to survive. The odds have always been against it, for it has been hunted almost to extinction and now its water holes are usurped by domestic flocks. Several large herds of Asiatic wild horses *Equus przevalskii przevalskii* Poliakoff have been built up in zoos in Europe and America but what their chances of survival would be if returned to their own native habitat, has yet to be discovered.

The Exmoor pony is descended from the Tarpan and has a family tree second to none as it represents a strain which came to the mainland of Britain whilst the country was still joined to the Continent c 12000 BC. Britain's emergence as an island, so isolating animal life, came about after the ice age when the

9

glaciers melted, the English Channel was formed and the Thames ceased to be a visible tributary of the Rhein. The Exmoor ponies, therefore, have a greater right to their native moor than any claim thought up by man.

On a sandbank called Sable Island, only two miles long by a mile wide, exposed to the gales of the Atlantic ocean, are to be found several herds, each with its own stallion, of possibly the toughest feral ponies in the world (see Plate 7). Their only grazing is the tough salt grass which also provides shelter. It is not clear how or exactly when the ancestors of the ponies arrived: they could have been survivors of a shipwreck since traces of many wrecks are to be found on the exposed sands, or they could have been purposely landed for use by the lighthouse keepers. Until caught for use, the Sable Island ponies are wild, free and yet also domesticated on their tiny stretch of native sands.

There is an agelessness in the scene of the herd of Shetland ponies on Mousa in the Shetland Islands group, for this picture could have been taken at any time during the past 2,000 years, had photography been invented. In all such isolated places, from Shetland to Antarctica, there seems to be no such thing as time. There is instead the simple natural rhythm of night and day and the passing seasons (see Plate 8).

We do not know how long such herds of ponies, almost unique in size, conformation and hardiness, have occupied their isolated habitat. The reason for their survival, despite the harshness of their environment, is that horses and ponies are probably the most versatile of all species of mammal, including man. For instance, if grazing is scarce they eat seaweed or even fish which local fishermen leave for them.

For centuries too, ponies have run wild on the Welsh Mountains, yet these ponies, wild though they may be, have unhappily learnt to distrust man. They have an instinctive fear of the mounted rider, two men on foot and two dogs (see Plate 10). Although not domesticated, probably not even feral, yet they have already acquired a knowledge and wariness of man's ungentle way of handling them.

All the so-called wild ponies in the British Isles actually belong to someone and, when still foals, are rounded up and branded, which must be a fairly unpleasant experience for a semi-wild animal. Contrary to popular belief, horses possess very long memories and are more than able to understand the relationship of cause and effect.

No longer wild but to some extent still free, the two-year old Posener colts in Plate 11 have just been let out to pasture and will return to their stalls at eventide. From the day they are weaned the horses are alloted their position at the manger in long, open sheds—both colts and fillies in their separate herds— and thus they soon have a friend on either side. They learn very quickly so that, within a few days, fifty entire colts will sort themselves out and find their proper place in the shed, waiting quietly for the groom to walk down the line and clip the rope to their headcollars. The step from freedom to domestication passes almost unnoticed by the youngsters themselves.

No horse ever loses the longing for freedom, and the beautiful dance into which the stallion in Plates 12–15 has flung himself with such splendid abandon, would do credit to Njinsky himself. These four pictures have produced four different positions of pure *joie de vivre*. Nothing is plainer than the horse's happiness at finding himself temporarily free and so he throws himself into a dance of sheer pleasure. Even the expressions on his face show that life is almost too good to be true and it is very seldom that the camera catches such moments in an animal's life. For these seconds, although domesticated, this stallion is truly wild and free.

Man has domesticated a number of formerly wild animals, but he has not demanded of any one of them as much as has been demanded of the horse, one of the fleetest of all living creatures: loyalty, obedience, endurance, complete subjection of its own natural instinct and adaptation to climate, food and human customs. So much is required of the horse and yet so often so little is given in return.

1 Wild Tarpan horses in the forest of Popielno *Equus przevalskii gmelini* Antonious

2 A herd of Achal Teké horses in the Kopet-Dag (Novosti Press Agency)

3 Horses of the 'Pogranichnik'
grazing in the Arasta Valley,
Tien Shan region (Norosti Press
Agency)

4 *Wild Horses in the Pampas* by Carlos Roume (Tryon Gallery Ltd)

5 The Asiatic wild horse *Equus przevalskii przevalskii* Poliakoff photographed in Rotterdam Zoo

6 A small herd of Exmoor ponies
on the moor

7 Ponies on Sable Island in the
Atlantic (Nova Scotia
Communications Information
Centre)

8 Herd of Shetland ponies on the Island of Mousa, Shetland with the 2000-year-old Pictish Broch in the background (Leslie Lane)

9 Highland ponies, Ross-shire

10 *The Repose and the Alarm—Welsh ponies in a Mountain Landscape* by J. F. Herring, 1854, owned by Mr and Mrs J. B. Sumner (Ackermann)

11 Herd of Posener Colts, Poland

12–15 Stallion executing a
freedom dance (Felizitas Tank)

2 Birth and Early Life

There are many factors in the creation and production of a good horse, the most important being the choice of the right parents and the right environment for the traumatic business of birth itself.

The preliminaries to giving birth are seen when the mare waxes, her teats are swollen and milk may be present. She is also restless, will 'walk her box' if stabled and roam restlessly around, if free, lying down only to get up again a moment later. The actual process of a normal birth, however, when the foal is lying in the proper position with the forefeet stretched out and head between the legs, is comparatively quick: the excellent pictures in Plates 16–19 show exactly how a foal is born.

Pony foals being more primitive, and thus nearer to nature, seem to have a better chance of survival, unlike the fashionable and 'civilised' breeds of horses which tend to acquire forms of neuroses. Many, if not all ponies, are bred under fairly natural conditions on the moors or mountains, leading a normal family life with the stallion always present. Pony studs usually keep a number of mares and foals together, although the stallion may not be allowed to run with them, and amongst the mares a very important social order is established and retained. Horses and cattle have a firmly established order of precedence which is of great importance to the psychological development of the animal. Once established, this order is never questioned and the animals live together in harmony and, as the saying goes, are good doers.

All fledglings and nestlings adopt the image of whichever species hatches them out, as anyone knows who has seen ducklings following a hen as their adopted mother. In the same way, a foal accepts the 'image of its own species' during the first two hours after birth. If its mother should die giving birth and the foal is then bottle-fed, it will accept humans as its own species and, later on, is even inclined to be frightened of other horses. A foal should have playmates of its own age and species if it is to develop as a temperamentally well balanced animal. Unfortunately, during the last few decades, the method of breeding warm-blood horses in some European countries (outside state studs) is undergoing a marked change which is not always for the better. There are, therefore, fewer opportunities for foals and young horses to be reared under psychologically normal conditions.

The Hanoverian mares shown in Plate 20 still belong to farmers with a traditional knowledge of breeding although in some circles the brood mare has sometimes become a hobby or status symbol. In reality of course, they are neither of these. They belong to a species which, essentially, needs space and a considerable amount of exercise. A mare and foal kept on an acre of paddock of not particularly good grass are so much out of their natural element that it is remarkable that so few 'rogue' horses are reared. Thankfully, this end result seems, in general, to be absent, but what is increasingly prevalent is the number of 'also rans' horses with no ambition, horses which cannot be produced above the norm. To succeed or to excel, horses must possess and be capable of showing, just that little bit extra.

The very young foal (see Plate 25) born on Christmas Eve 1974, to Anemone the Trakehner mare, comes from a line of horses which, on the dam's side, has endured more than any other breed of horses. This foal's granddam, Adana, as a yearling, completed the long trek of 900 miles from her home-land in East Prussia to Western Germany in the winter of 1944–45, as described in my book, *Flight of the East Prussian Horses*.

Some part-time breeders regard the Trakehner as the status symbol already mentioned, with the result that neuroses are being bred into this once-hardy and extremely good tempered breed. The mistake lies more in the *method* of breeding and could be corrected by the formation of 'co-operative' studs so that the mares and foals could lead the normal lives denied them in the one-box, acre-paddock existence.

In England, equally unfortunate methods are used by breeders who cross large stallions on small mares with the hope of getting larger foals. Since the mare largely determines the size of the foal this unwise practice has no advantages whatever, and should cease, both for the sake of the mare herself and for the foal which may well have difficulty in suckling when born of unequal sized parents. The offspring of genuine pony parents have no trouble for they are almost always born small. When holding their heads in the natural position they can easily reach the mare's udder and the teat fits neatly into the groove made by the foal's tongue. Larger foals have to bend their necks at an unnatural angle.

Living as a member of a herd teaches young horses many things which help enormously later on when it is time for them to be brought into the stable and trained. Their attitude is co-operative and, from playing constant games and chasing around with others of their own age, they are fitter and more mentally alert. Curiously, too, they have learnt the old axiom of doing unto others . . . , whereas an only foal has never had occasion to learn that a kick hurts and that play battles have rules. Such a foal knows nothing about discipline and his chances of making 'a good 'un' are that much more remote.

As soon as it is weaned, if not before, the foal has to learn the discipline of domestication. It has to accept a head-collar and learn to be led around, and to obey orders whether it likes it or not. Although there is little pain, clearly no foal relishes being branded as shown in Plate 27. A willingness to accept the 'rules' devised by humans is a big step forward in the education of a six-month old foal, as is the shattering experience of separation from its mother. Both foal and mare can, and sometimes do suffer emotionally, but the trauma of this experience is considerably lessened if the foal has playmates whilst still running with his dam, and if the mare too, belongs to a herd of mares separated from their foals at about the same time.

The early life of the species *Equus* is all too short and the young horse must grow up very quickly. The period of foalhood lasts a bare twelve months, and Thoroughbred horses, for instance, are broken-in, trained and ready to race at two years. This particular breed, however, is bred to mature early. The foals of most other breeds are slower in reaching maturity but consequently have longer working lives.

Language is part of the process of development which commences as soon as the foal is born, so both language and the language of signs is common to all species. Horses have a wider range of communication than is, perhaps, generally realised and also a greater level of intelligence than they are usually credited with. They learn to understand the meaning of vocal sounds given by man as well as the reaction expected when he uses the so-called aids, including the different reactions to leg pressure from a mounted rider.

Horses do talk to each other and to people by sounds emitted from their throats. There is the friendly nicker or whicker of greeting and the entirely different neighs of hunger, surprise or greeting when the recipient is some distance away. Other sounds are the shrill yell of anger, the soft, almost imperceptable whisper of a mare to her foal, the whinny of pleasure from a stallion to a mare and the squeal of annoyance from her if she rejects his advances. The horse's low groans and sighs of pain vary little from those of the human, and human sympathy under these circumstances is as easily understood by the sick animal.

Dreaming, although rarely witnessed, follows the same process with horses as with humans. The eyes close, the head nods, muscles of the face twitch and short, sharp whinnies are accompanied by grunts, squeals or neighs. The horse is obviously living or re-living an event which is as real to him as to a human talking in his sleep.

In addition to the sound of its voice, the horse can communicate by various language signs (see *The Language of the Horse* by M. Schaeffer). If the teeth are shown and the ears laid back, the horse is angry; if the ears are pricked forward and the nostrils held in the direction of 'winding' or inspecting an object, curiosity is shown. Horses can wear expressions of pleasure, tiredness, stubbornness, sickness, wickedness or mischievousness—although humour is not common to all horses or ponies, and as later pictures show, horses engaged in great effort wear expressions of great concentration. At times, foals wear expressions of submission, thus acknowledging the

26

superiority of a higher ranking horse. The swishing of the tail and stamping of a hind leg are warnings; pawing with a forefoot is usually a sign of impatience or boredom, and rolling is one of physical enjoyment. Mutual nibbling of the skin is also an activity of enjoyment although it can also be designated as 'grooming'.

All these signs and expressions are understood by other horses, and indeed by cattle that share grazing with horses which are, in all instances, their superiors in rank. They should be understood too by humans and, in the case of great horsemen, always are.

It is not true to say that animals do not suffer. The mare shown in Plate 28 is as uncomfortable in her pregnancy as any human would be in a similar situation—an unborn foal can make life very tiring and troublesome for its mother-to-be.

It is because horses have these physical and psychological feelings and reactions that they have evolved and *survived* over so many millions of years. As a species, where other species failed, they were able to develop a versatility. They moved with the times and developed their own ways of dealing with life's problems. Horses are not dependent upon any one climate, environment or sustenance. Equally important, they possess *independent* characters.

People who make silly remarks like 'he jumps because he's too stupid not to', or 'he knows he would hurt his legs if he didn't', are not fit to have the association or care of a horse. No horse can be made to jump if he does not want to. Indeed, he cannot be made to do anything he does not want to do, but the thousands of years of evolution and domestication have taught horses that survival depends upon versatility, and they are intelligent enough to have learnt co-operation with the many thousands of societies and tribes with which they have come into contact—a process of development which many human beings are in very grave danger of losing. Horses may not be clever but many are surely wise. If we can only respect this wisdom and learn to bring out the horse's independence to help us achieve our ambitions, whatever they may be, then we are really a partnership.

16 The miracle of birth has begun

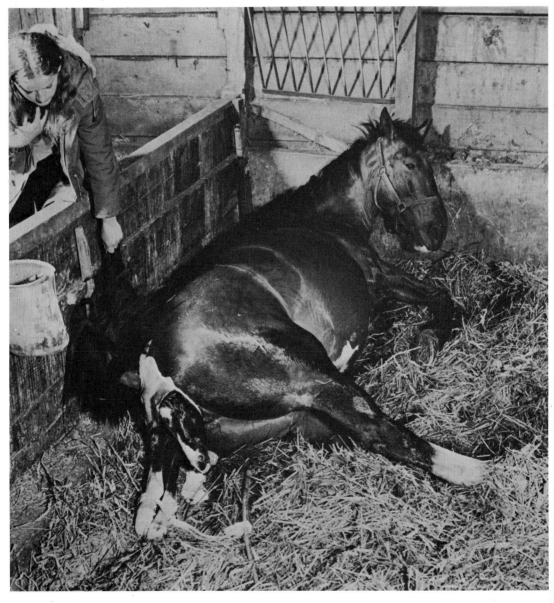

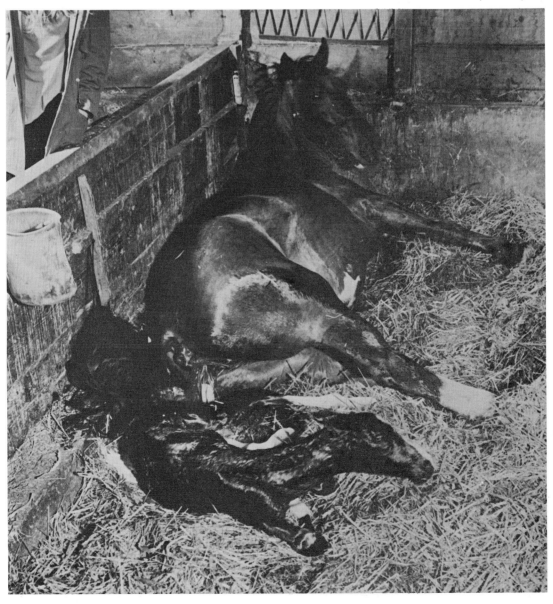

17 A new member of the horse tribe breathes independently

18 And a proud mare sniffs and
licks her new-born baby

19 Within a few moments the
foal is on his feet looking for
milk (The mare was
photographed by Wim Koch
and owned by A. P. J. van der
Woyden, Zevenhoven)

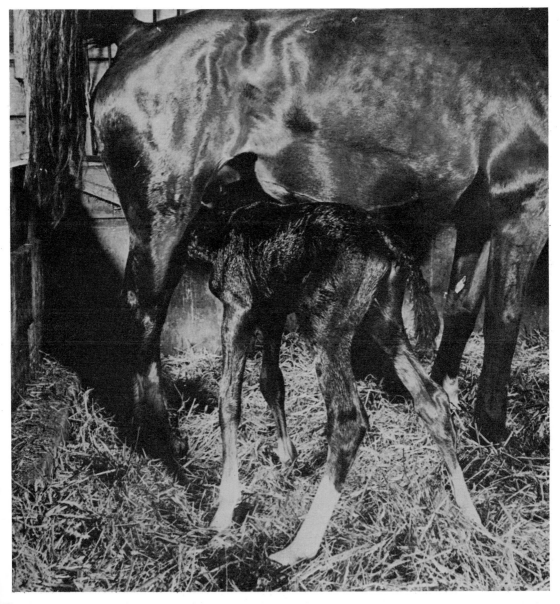

20 One family of Hanoverian
mares

HRH the Duke of Edinburgh
competing in a driving marathon
at the Royal Windsor Show
(Syndication International)

Canadian chuckwaggon horses act upon a split-second decision
(Spectrum Colour Library)

21 Fjord pony mare and foal, Norway (Leslie Lane)

Horses in Lake Geneva Region (Swiss National Tourist Office)

22 Welsh mare and foal

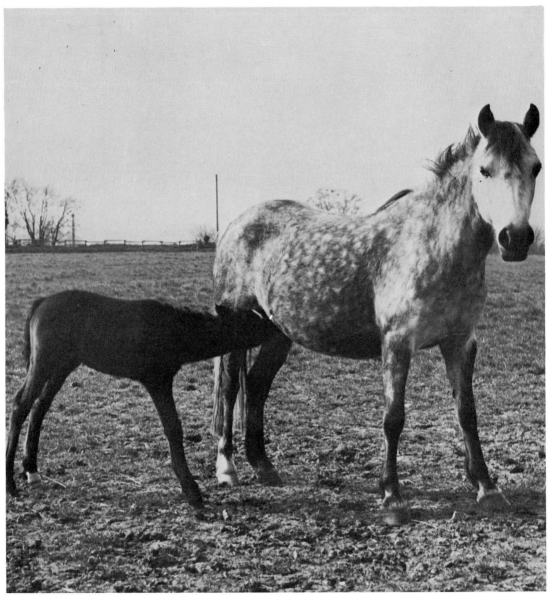

23 Hanoverian mare and foal.

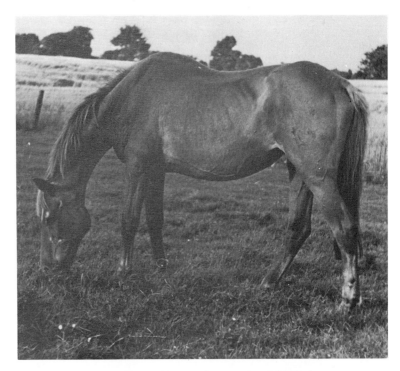

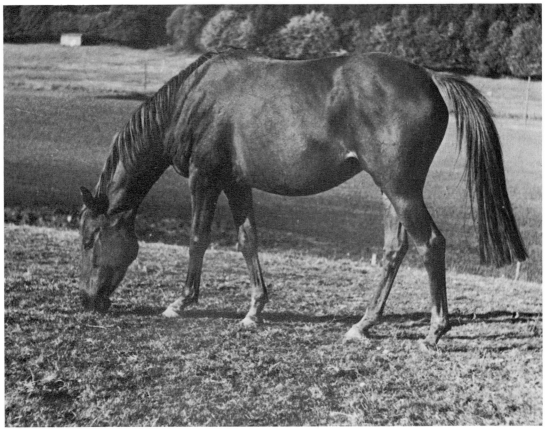

25 A very young foal looks out
on the world (Felizitas Tank)

26 Ambrosius, three-year-old great-grandson of the Trakehner mare Adana (Felizitas Tank)

28 An aged in-foal mare

29 Arabian mares, Janow
Podlaski, Poland

30 Arabian Stallion, Janow
Podlaski, Poland

31 Three-year-old Masurian
fillies at Liski in the former
Province of East Prussia

32 There are strict rules to all
fighting games (Felizitas Tank)

33 I always said you'd catch
your death . . . (Felizitas Tank)

35 To our mutual satisfaction . . .
(Felizitas Tank)

36 But I will not tolerate
impertinence (Felizitas Tank)

34 Conversation between
mother and daughter (Felizitas
Tank)

Camargue horses enjoying their freedom (Spectrum Colour Library)

Two horses meet (Felizitas Tank)

Tired from playing (Felizitas Tank)

HM the Queen taking the salute on Burmese at the Trooping of the Colour (Peter Roberts)

A Hanoverian stallion gives an exhibition of long-reining at Celle

37 For the very young foal, life is full of surprises! For the first time the foal sees the mare rolling and this causes it to gallop round her

38 It always itches just where
one can't reach it (Felizitas Tank)

A unique picture of a foal rolling
(Felizitas Tank)

39 One has to have a purpose in
life!

40 But a lot of sleep is needed too!

41 To sleep—to dream—to be

3 Relationships and Training

Most people who know horses, will grant that many horses and most ponies do possess to a lesser or greater degree 'the quality of being wise'. Yet this quality is neither conscious nor acquired by learning as in the case of mankind but is an inner quality.

The tolerance of the species *Equus* towards the species *Homo sapiens* is remarkable. The illustrations in this book show only a fraction of the horse's willingness to co-operate in a variety of activities which must, at times, appear to him to be quite extraordinary. Occasionally, when handling or working horses one is given a glimmer of the horse's opinion of these activities, but wisely he usually says nothing and continues to do as he is bid, not because he has not the power to refuse and not because his survival through thousands of years has always depended upon co-operation with man, but because versatility is a part of equine wisdom. Indeed most of the time the horse is trying to understand what man wants—only sometimes does man try to understand his horse.

The horse's ears are often a barometer of his understanding. What he *hears* considerably affects his concentration and his hearing is very acute. It has been said that the wave of sound from the crowd at the finish of a big race can stop a horse in his tracks. For some horses it is as if a barrier has suddenly fallen and very often the leading horse will unaccountably swerve or slow down.

In training for dressage or school work, as shown in Plate 42, the horse is listening for the slightest indication and is concentrating upon every movement and sound made by its partner. Only by appreciating that the rider is one half of a partnership and by *acting* as a partner, can man fully succeed in obtaining a horse's confidence and ultimately its co-operation in successful endeavour.

The two delightful illustrations of the four year-old Trakehner stallion Vizier, show him flirting with his owner after a Hubertus Meet, in Schleswig-Holstein (see Plates 43 and 44). The half-closed eyes lit with a sparkle, accompanied by this expressive movement of his lips—called in German 'flehmen'—is almost sublime. Vizier bears out everything that can be said on the unique confidence that exists between horse and rider in a successful partnership.

When such a partnership is broken, which often happens when a horse is sold, I wonder what goes on inside the mind of the animal. He must and certainly does feel the parting from his rider as much as from his home surroundings. Suddenly the familiar has vanished, and it is a matter of extraordinary good fortune if the new owner is as sympathetic as he has been used to. The horse must start all over again in his attempt to 'get through' to this new, unknown human entity.

We know what the physical language barrier alone can do to human relationships. What happens when the language of the horse can only be expressed in the way he looks and so tries to show what he is perhaps feeling? His previous owner knew that twitching ears meant: 'I am tired, give me a nice straw bed'. The new owner may *think* that twitching ears means bad-temper or unwillingness and so react accordingly. Instead of a mutual confidence which could lead to co-operation, exactly the opposite occurs, lack of communication, misunderstanding and distrust.

Almost every horse in the world has changed hands once and many quite often. Whether the new horse really possesses the attributes to 'fit the bill', or whether the new purchaser simply imagines that it has—on this alone the future of a pony or horse at an auction hangs (see Plate 45).

On the other hand, occasionally, a badly handled horse finds himself unexpectedly in the possession of an owner with real fellow-feeling, or *sympathie*—a word which, in German, means *mysterious, miraculous*—then this partnership between horse and rider can indeed be almost a miracle. Those people who can 'do anything with horses' simply have this fellow-feeling which is immediately communicated to the animal.

My sister, Vivien Boon, has always had this gift of communication. Many years ago now, my father bought a point-to-point mare who enjoyed the graphic name of Ratty Rose which she fully lived up to. She was apparently both a man-hater and, reputedly, a man-eater as well. On arrival she was promptly turned loose in the horse-yard and, for about a week, suffered solitary confinement, being fed through the manger hatch. Then the day arrived when my father decided to try her out and one of the men was asked to catch her. Ratty Rose was as wild as the proverbial bronco, presenting a pair of very active heels every time the man approached. My sister, then aged seven, calmly announced that she could catch her, despite the fact that we children had all been forbidden to go near the mare. Taking the head-collar she climbed into the manger through the feed hatch and called to Ratty Rose who, with the docility of a pet lamb, walked up to the manger and put her head into the head-collar!

Years later we had a horse in the yard which had supposedly killed one man and almost destroyed another. In order to break its spirit—it was fashionable at one time to *break* horses—the wretched animal had been starved and was a miserable sight. We stabled him in a small yard and Vivien personally fed and talked to the horse regularly for about a month. One day at a meet of foxhounds, the previous owner asked how the horse was getting on, to be told that he was looking better and eating well. 'In that case', he insisted, 'you'll never do anything with him'. 'I have never ridden a horse that was not fed, and when he's ready, I'll bring him out', my sister replied. When she did, the horse turned out to be a perfectly ordinary well mannered hunter.

Horses recognise a very marked order of precedence or rank, especially those kept in herds. This may seem to go against the idea of an equal partnership evolving between a good horse and an understanding rider. In fact, this is not the case, for the extraordinary horse always belongs to the higher rank of the herd and has to be partnered by a rider who can give it the feeling that he or she is superior in rank. If the rider cannot instill this confidence into his mount then the best horse in the world will never be able to give his best. The average horse which, despite the right breeding, good health and expert training, still does not shine, naturally belongs to the lower levels of the hierarchy of the herd.

A horse's confidence begins to grow at a very early age amongst their friends and, if it is not destroyed, it is carried with them through life and goes a long way towards the creation of an outstanding horse. The foal on the left of plate 41 developed into an international show jumper and represented her country. Having herself borne a foal at twenty-eight years of age, she will surely be alive and well at thirty summers. She and her owner have been partners all their lives and, although her home surroundings have changed, the general environment that surrounded her activities has remained the same.

The horse needs the same kind of confidence in his rider to perform safely and competently in the circus ring, and to 'die' Hungarian style with his rider cracking a stock whip over his head. This same feeling applies to the three-year-old grey Hanoverian colt cantering through the woodlands at Wester-celle. Due to careful training, life is still truly good. The young horse enjoys his cross-country test before a final veterinary examination to confirm his future at stud. The young groom will remain with the stallion throughout his stud career, so the entire always has a friend at hand. Although often not recognised in our over-civilised societies, this fact alone helps towards developing a good horse.

Confidence is essential between the farrier and the horse he is shoeing. The former could ruin the horse by inept workman-ship and the horse, with a well directed kick, could certainly handicap the farrier. It takes very little time for a young horse to learn that well shod feet are a necessity along the stony pathways of life. Nothing is more unnatural, if one thinks about it, than for a horse to put up with the paring of his feet, the fitting of a red-hot shoe and the nailing on of the cold iron. But here again, is an example of the horse's versatility and intuitive wisdom.

The pictures of the bull fight and the *charreada* show activities which I consider to be an abuse of the relationship between horse and rider. It is quite unnatural for a horse to submit to being chased by a bull (which is inferior in rank, anyway) no matter how skillfully his rider directs him to avoid injury, and the expression on the horse's face gives the lie to any form of confidence or co-operation. This is even more the case in the *charreada* in Plate 53.

Quite probably, horses have no objection to chasing cattle which are, as I have already said, of a lower rank, since this activity mostly takes place in the wide, open spaces. But the abuse of confidence must be acute when the rider demands that his horse should aid him in bullying a small defenceless member of its own species.

Training on the lunge—detail from painting of Messenger Boy, winner Hackney Horse Show, London 1905 (Commercial Studios, Ipswich)

61

42 Enormous concentration is required. Goldlack, ridden by Lockie Richards of New Zealand, performs a half-pass (Alix Coleman)

43–4 Vizier, a four-year-old entire flirts with his owner Frl Erdmute von Zitzewitz (Felizitas Tank)

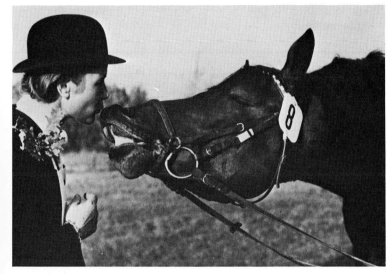

46 There are occasions when
training can be a real pleasure

45 Tullow Fair, Ireland painted
by Sarah Ponsonby. Will the
change be for the better?
(Cuming Wright-Watson
Associates Limited)

47 The Croupade, a movement
performed by a horse of the
Spanish High School (Leslie Lane)

49 Confidence is of the first
importance (Douglas Dickins
FRPS)

50 An incredible exhibition of
absolute trust (Leslie Lane)

51 The farrier is one of the most
important men in a horse's life

53 What goes on in the minds of these men and their unwilling partners? (Mexican Tourist Office)

54–5 Relationships matter very much

56 Size is no matter, it is personality that counts (*Daily Mirror*)

57 Time to celebrate Christmas (Felizitas Tank)

4 Competition

The late Col Jack Hance, one of Britain's greatest riding masters, used to insist that 'only the great are humble'. Great horsemen and women have always shown humility towards their even greater partners, since after all it is the *horse* which succeeds in performing a breath-catching test, in beating those flying seconds on the race-course or across country, or in leaping higher than any other horse in show jumping competitions and so on. Without a good helping of humility, riders will not have the patience necessary to discipline themselves and their horses to the hours, days, months and even years of training necessary to reach the top. Humility and patience are also essential, of course, to face the many frustrations too when success is elusive.

We tend to overlook the stress and strain endured by the numerous horses that are driven from show to show and race meeting to race meeting. The show jumpers, in particular, often travel hundreds of miles a week and, whilst the rider can relax and even sleep during these journeys, the horses must travel standing on their four feet. How tiring it must be too, to cope with the different temperatures of heat, cold and even rain when they are flown from one hemisphere to another, and *then* have to face the stark reality of difficult fences in a strange arena before a vast and noisy crowd. How they must long for home and a quiet paddock! Horses are temperamentally bound to a habitat and their ability to cope with abrupt changes in their accustomed rhythm again testifies to their remarkable versatility.

Almost without exception the great international horses like Idle Dice and Snowbound of the USA, or Simona of West Germany, to mention only three out of dozens, constantly give of their best and, if they have not been brought on too fast but have been allowed time for both their characters and physical abilities to develop, they do succeed, becoming outstanding horses which remain at the top of their fields for many years.

The public too, takes a lot for granted from the horses they watch. Even the commentator, instead of explaining the skill of the horse and the real but frequently overlooked art of the horse and rider partnership, wallows in clichés the only merit of which is his own flair for adjectives. I am often reminded of the circuses of ancient Rome, wondering how many more bodies will be thrown to the lions or how many more horses will be overfaced by the magnitude of the fences. There seem to be no limits in our civilised society when it comes to pandering to the spectacular, no limits to trying to make a brave horse jump higher and bigger. Only occasionally does a great rider like Hans Günther Winkler retire himself and his horse from a *barrage*, and all too often, the consideration behind such a gesture passes unnoticed by the majority of spectators.

A number of pointless expressions such as 'I asked him . . .' have crept into our equine language. Of course, no rider *asks* a horse anything, but indicates by his aids that some particular movement is required. If the aid is correct then the trained horse responds but should it be incorrect, and frequently with the less than top-class rider aids are given either at the split-second wrong moment, incorrectly, or not at all, then the trained horse will invariably ignore the aid and achieve the desired result. The untrained horse obeys the faulty aid and mistakes result, for which, more often than not the horse is blamed.

A properly schooled, fit, intelligent horse is just as keen to be successful as his rider. On being awarded a red rosette many horses look around at the crowd of spectators in expectation of the applause. I am sure that all trained horses are quite aware that a clear round in a jumping competition is the objective and that great horses will try to achieve this aim. There would appear to be no doubt in Neptune's mind that he is fully aware of his achievement (see Plate 60). Few of us have the privilege and ability to chalk up a first in sport and fewer still who do so have started off with the handicap of a disability. Due to war-time conditions, Neptune developed ricketts as a foal, which appeared as a bony tissue enlargement on the near fetlock—a razor's breadth separating the enlargement from the joint, which had it touched it would have caused immobility. Neptune, however, achieved what had not been considered possible. He was the first horse in the world to be placed in, and subsequently to win an Olympic Horse Trial at Harewood in 1953, who was trained and ridden by a woman. Neptune was certainly in every sense a great horse. He stood 17 hh and was a great jumper—he cleared thirty-two measured feet at Badminton in 1948, whilst at show jumping he had already won a high jump competition. He could never be held but he was a good listener.

Every good harness horse too, listens for the voice, and reacts to a split-second command. The harness horse's listening has to be even more concentrated because his partner's voice is that much further away—he cannot 'feel' the whip (coachman) in the same way and with the same closeness as he could 'feel' a rider. I am sure, therefore, that there is an even greater *rapport* between a whip and his team than between most riders and their horses, although the affinity and unity between a top event or show jumping rider and his or her horse is obviously very remarkable.

It clearly requires tremendous listening concentration in the hubbub and din of the race to hear the voice of the driver of a Chuckwaggon (see Plate 64) and yet the last team responds to split-second commands to avoid a collision. The pacing trotters (see Plate 65) driven to sulkies, racing at Charlottetown, Prince Edward Island, Canada are also listening as can be seen from the position of the ears—that barometer of concentration, referred to in the last chapter.

Plates 68 and 69 are a real contrast in concentration and lack of it, in co-operation and non-co-operation. The heavyweight hunter Fair Gin, shown by John Hollowell, is surely asking if his position is *absolutely* correct. He is ready to change his stance, should his rider give the slightest hint, a horse trained to obey and yet capable of galloping across country in the wake of hounds, using his own judgement to negotiate fences safely without injury to his rider. In absolute contrast is the second horse, an unbroken *grullo* mustang, whose sole objective is to get shot of his unwanted load at the first and fastest possible moment—in less than the eight second limit. The rider, meanwhile, has only balance and rowelled spurs to help him stay on board.

The great steeplechaser, Red Rum, needs no introduction to enthusiastic supporters of steeplechasing. This exceptional horse has twice won the Grand National, one of the few to do so, and this puts him into a class of his own. These National Hunt Steeplechasers possess enormous courage, a characteristic of many breeds of horses, and a great willingness to co-operate with their trainers and jockeys. In addition to this, they have both the ability and stamina to jump a course of thirty-two very stiff fences over a distance of four miles.

The horses galloping from Kyz-kun (see Plate 71) have an expression of uncertainty on their faces as well they might, since the young man having failed to kiss the girl in full gallop is being soundly beaten for his failure!

Plate 73 is a very unusual photograph of a thirteen-in-hand or team of Gelderland horses to a Drag. The Gelderland is Holland's most famous breed of harness horse but it is equally at home under the saddle and as a show jumper. This team in particular is now well known in Holland. Extremely spectacular visually, this picture represents both skill and obedience. The skill of the whip is tremendous, for the weight of the reins alone is more than most men can lift and hold for any length of time, but his skill would be nothing if the man on the box seat could not obtain obedience and immediate response from his horses. Here, this large team is going forward with every indication of enjoyment but when I was visiting studs in Poland, I was told of the occasion when a team of fifteen stallions were shown to a carriage and, though they did not actually get out of hand, they got into a gallop and could not be stopped by the coachman. The second coachman had to help on the reins before the team could be brought to a halt. The Poles hereafter decided that a team of thirteen-in-hand would be the largest to be shown, though in Holland and West Germany at Celle different teams can be seen at shows.

Another delightful example of the horse's natural willingness to co-operate are Gelderlanders (Plate 74) being inspected for the Stud Book: the ridden saddle horse, the harness horse to a gig and the young horse led in-hand. The saddle horse, standing quietly and correctly and ridden in a snaffle bit looks at the judge with interest. The harness horse, standing 'four-square' and with neck flexed would be a delight to drive, whilst the horse in-hand wonders what will be expected of him next. All the horses have their ears pricked and the turn-out of all three appears to be perfect. Such combination classes might prove of interest to horse shows outside the Netherlands: the horses would clearly have to be shown as a team and judged as such.

The competing horsemen of Morocco and Sumba appear to have failed to inspire their mounts who look dull and listless. Yet, surprisingly in view of this, it is said of Sumba, an island belonging to the Indonesian group, that it is 'governed by the horse'—equine motives are even woven into capes and shawls worn by both men and women.

All the foregoing illustrations are of horses trained for different kinds of competition. They have been schooled by a wide variety of methods under widely differing circumstances and each is successful in its individual sphere. The Hanoverian mare Simona, ridden by Hartwig Steenken, see page 102, was certainly in the world champion class, and in 1975 at 17 years of age was retired to stud. When she was originally sold at the annual auction at Verden in the autumn of 1962, she was described in the protocol as: 'very well behaved, reliable, concentrates on her work. Very active, excellent action, willing to do everything asked of her and a comfortable ride. Jumps high and wide like a rubber ball at all heights and can take off at any approach. She rarely makes a fault. A first-class jumper'.

Count von Thun-Hohenstein, the well known German authority described her farewell appearance in the following way: 'As Simona in her shining satin coat danced out of the ring to a happy, peaceful retirement, perhaps a few people remembered, for a few seconds, the fate of hundreds of thousands of so-called sporting horses of every description, who just as loyally and patiently gave their best for the pleasure and ambition of mankind, and who later suffered a dreary end to their lives'.

58 Rodney Jenkins, the top US
professional on Idle Dice, winner
of $100,000 in prize money, the
American record (E. D. Lacey)

60 To be the first in the world
does not come to everyone.
Neptune and his owner (Monty)

61 Training in obedience at the
Burghley Horse Trials

62 A three-year-old entire at
Westercelle, West Germany

63 A Shetland pony team having fun (*Birmingham Post and Mail*)

63 A Shetland pony team having fun (*Birmingham Post and Mail*)

65 Sulky trotting race in Prince Edward Island, Canada (Peter Roberts)

66 Two famous trotters of bygone days. Shepheard F. Knapp became one of the most famous trotters in the US

64 Chuckwaggon race (Peter Roberts)

67 The ball's there—who will get in first? (Mike Roberts)

69 Freedom is a thing called
'getting rid of one's rider'
(Douglas Dickins)

68 Am I standing just right?
Heavyweight Hunter Fair Gin
with John Hollowell in the
saddle (Leslie Lane)

70 Red Rum jumping Beechers,
Grand National, 1974—one of
the greatest ever steeplechasers
(E. G. Byrne)

71 In Kyz-Kun, a Kazak mounted
competition (Novosti Press
Agency)

72 Gold Rod, a golden palomino, bred in America, a winner of many classes (Eugene Belt)

73 Team of 13 in hand.
Tremendous obedience and
concentration is needed from
all the horses (Stamboek Bureau)

74 A class with a difference—
trio of Gelderland horses
(Stamboek Bureau)

75 Sumba ponies in Indonesia
(Vendla V. Langenn)

5 Pleasure and Pageantry

Pleasure and pageantry seem to go hand-in-hand. The gorgeous showmanship of royal pageantry when the Windsor Greys, following the royal tradition of the Hanoverian Creams of two centuries ago, draw the British coronation coach, gives pleasure to many thousands of people. The Creams were, incidentally, introduced into the British tradition by George I, Elector of Hanover and bred by the Electress Sophie, his mother.

The Trooping of the Colour, or Royal Ascot, are just two of many traditional occasions when the lives of ordinary people are cheered by the spectacular and united in the feeling of participation. Such events in which horses play the leading rôle are rare, even though the people of the British Isles have a thousand years of tradition behind them. In the past, many more horses were used but now their numbers have decreased, so let us encourage the use of horses for ceremonial occasions for the sake of the splendour and nobility they lend them.

Let us also defend the racing of that unique breed, the Thoroughbred on famous courses like Ascot, against those small-time economists whose ideas bring neither pageantry nor pleasure to the paying public.

The Thoroughbred has been exported to many foreign countries but Ascot, the shop window of British racing, is where it is seen at its magnificent best. Fashions, foibles and champagne may be in evidence and be decried by the aforesaid small-time economists, but what is perhaps not so obvious is the prestige value of this great race—not only the export value of the horses, but its importance in the eyes of the guests who attend such race meetings simply to watch almost perfect horses racing against each other. Great horses from the Continent and the USA race there and, such is the value of these animals, the British National Stud, with the help of his Italian owner, has purchased Grundy, winner of the 1975 Derby, so that the stallion's progeny may influence future stock.

No particular strain or breed of horses is more suitable than any other for ceremonial pageantry. Suitability springs mainly from temperament. However, some strains have developed placid dispositions encouraged by generations of selective breeding, and among these are the Lipizzaner horses whose ancestors helped institute the pageantry of chivalry (see Plates 47 and 48). Clearly, quietness of temperament is of great importance, but sobriety should never be obtained by the use of drugs. If the horse is temperamentally unsuited for the work required of it, it should be moved on so that other talents which it may well possess can be used elsewhere. There is nothing very clever in riding or using a drugged horse and in some instances it can be extremely dangerous.

Sir Alfred Munnings RA has caught on canvas a different kind of pageantry in his picture of trees in parkland and a white Highland pony called Jock carrying the late King George V. Throughout history and in ancient history, it is clear that white horses have enjoyed a privileged position in the minds of men. The inhabitants of ancient Central Asia considered them to be holy, revering them as lesser gods, and a great number were stabled in the temples of Assur the ancient capital of Assyria.

It often seems that incredibly hard work and ambition make up the greater part of the mutual sharing of effort in competitive events or sports—fun and enjoyment seem to find little part in the proceedings. However, there are many other forms of riding and work with horses which are solely pleasurable. Over the years, the horse has played a key part in man's enjoyment of sporting activities. Hawking is a very ancient sport and its popularity probably spread from Scythia through Tartary, Persia and Asia Minor to North Africa. From the mounted nomads of Asia to the Bedouin tribes of Africa, both the hawk and falcon were necessary to the skill and enjoyment of a sport which was shared by the horse. The early Egyptians trained hawks to falconry many centuries BC and we can assume that the sport was enjoyed in all North African countries (see Plate 82). This horse is a typical Berber and from the keen look in his eye, it is as interested in its master's sport as the Moor himself. The Berber, more commonly and incorrectly known as the Barb horse, is bred throughout Northern and Central African countries and as far south as the Sudan, and there are a number of different strains of the breed.

The object of riding horses for pleasure must be that both parties should enjoy the exercise, as are these riders and their mounts trekking in Glen Amble, Strathyre (see Plate 85). One of the most pleasurable experiences is to ride in snow or to drive a horse to a sleigh. I recall riding my Thoroughbred, Silver Spring, on a bright moonlit night when a heavy fall of snow was covering our country lanes. The sky was indigo blue with the stars brightly twinkling. Not a sound could be heard except the horse's muffled action as we cantered along.

Driving a really good harness pony or cob is an equally pleasurable pastime. In these days of over-filled roads, the harness horse must be absolutely bomb-proof, to cope with the unexpected, and traffic-proof, to cope with the rush of noise and movement caused by lorries and cars. Horses are harnessed and driven according to the different usages in their various countries as, for example, the Russian troika pulled by grey Orloff Trotters (see Plate 87). Despite the name, only the centre horse should trot. The outside horses canter, and to help them the head is bent slightly outwards by drawing the rein a little tighter, thus throwing the horse onto his near or off foreleg. The horses do not wear blinkers and so can see all around them.

They wear breast harness and only the centre horse is between shafts. Troika racing is popular in Russia and the Orloff Trotter, which has been bred for over two centuries, is the most popular breed of harness horse.

Plates 89–91 represent three countries of the world—the UK, the German Federal Republic, and the People's Republic of Poland—each with its own language and form of government. Yet the people of all these countries have one thing at least in common—their interest and affection for horses. James Pollard's painting of London's busy Piccadilly includes four strains of horses: the Yorkshire Coach horse with Thoroughbred blood, the tradesman's cob, the useful Roadster and the harness pony. The pair of dark brown Hanoverian stallions in Plate 91 await their master, the director of the State Stud at Celle, whilst their sons are being tested across country. The picture in Plate 89 of the pair of grey Anglo-Arabs was taken when I was in Poland officially visiting the State Studs there and I had the pleasure of driving this pair through the magnificent forests of Masuria, formerly the Province of East Prussia.

Plate 92 shows a German mounted policeman mounted on a weight-carrying Hanoverian gelding. Although police horses in West Germany are a fast disappearing race, there are still large areas, like the Lüneberger Heide, where motorised patrol cars are unable to travel. In this case, pleasure and duty are combined for horse and man—this rider even kept the horse at his own expense to help him patrol his district. Some countries, including many metropolitan areas of the British Isles, still retain mounted police patrols.

Police horses are generally of the middle to heavy-weight type, with impeccable manners, completely obedient and reliable. Their characters and characteristics are similar to those of the Windsor Greys and indeed are the qualities which are looked for in all the horses used for pleasure and pageantry—staid enough to transport a monarch, sensible enough to stand firm in front of a riot, yet gay enough to enjoy the crowds, the pomp and ceremony, and to perform their work with a will.

77 The Coronation: horses contribute to the spectacle of a royal occasion (Hulton Picture Library)

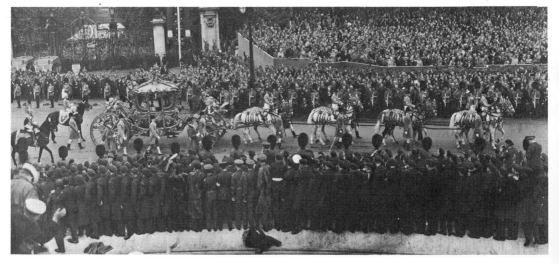

The great trek of refugees in the
winter of 1944–5, painted by
Heinz Düllberg

78 The state coach of Hanover
with the famous Cream horses
(by kind permission of HRH the
Prince of Hanover, Duke of
Brunswick and Lüneburg)

79 The Mews, Buckingham
Palace. Rest from State
occasions (*Sport and General*)

The immortal Simona (*Sport and
General*)

80 Time to stand and time to
think

81 *HM King George V riding
'Jock'* by Sir A. J. Munnings RA
(Ipswich Museum Committee)

82 A Berber horseman flies his
falcon—the artist has caught the
horse's keen interest in the
proceedings

83 *Top:* A quatriga (Foto vision)

84 A most skilful exhibition of driving for pleasure (Foto vision)

85 Pony trekkers in Glen Amble, Scotland (Leslie Lane)

86 *Orloff Trotter* by
N. Schwerchkoff (Novosti Press
Agency)

87 Troika in the snow (Novosti Press Agency)

88 Sleighs waiting at Arosta
(Novosti Press Agency)

89 Part bred Arabs in the forests
of Eastern Poland

90 Horses were a part of
everyday life 150 years ago

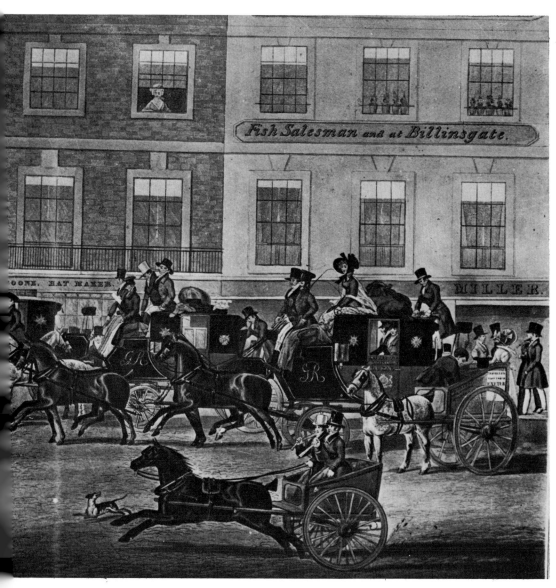

91 And in some countries they are today a part of everyday life. W Germany Stallion trials at Westercelle

92 German policeman in the
Lüneburg Heide

93 British Police horses

Entrants in the Montreux Festival
(Swiss National Tourist Office)

94 Fun is fun no matter how young—or old one happens to be (Stanley Hurwitz)

95 Hightime at Wembley (Monty)

6 At Work

All the characteristics listed as essential for pageantry horses, are required for 'working' horses or ponies and many more besides. *None of the glory but all of the sweat* is theirs, and by their labour many generations of families have been fed, warmed, transported and saved from sinking ships. In most cases man's pleasure is a horse's work, and for centuries man's very existence in peace and war has been dependent upon the working horse. This chapter, therefore, contains a large proportion of illustrations which show horses helping to make man's life easier. Quite possibly many horses enjoy the work they have to do, come wet or fine, in good health or poor condition, whilst some tolerate it because there is no way out, and a few will demonstrate quite plainly that they hate it.

The horses of Malta and Ireland (see Plate 96) possibly lead a fairly easy life transporting visitors on pleasurable outings around the islands. I have always understood that cobs and ponies enjoy a view and will come to a halt on reaching the summit of a hill in order to look around them. If they are not overworked by holidaymakers with too little knowledge of horse-keeping, caravanning, for instance, can provide a delightful holiday for both horse and man. True gipsy horses too, may not fare so badly (see Plate 99). However, when it comes to harvesting the fruits of the sea and land the work becomes harder and the cob, by selective breeding, has developed into a powerful mass of bone and muscle. Crab-fishing off the coast of Flanders (see Plate 100) needs a strong, hard horse to stand up to wind and water from above and below.

Pit-ponies, by comparison, had to be small, nimble, yet very strong and courageous. All their lives were spent working below ground and some were still being used in British mines as recently as 1971. The day of the pit pony is now over as coal mines are completely mechanised. The ponies, wearing protective face-guards, must have moved millions of tons of coal. They rarely came to the surface until their life's work was finished, apart from the annual mine holidays when the ponies enjoyed two weeks of rest in the open air where they were justly pampered by local village children.

As recently as 150 years ago in Britain, pack ponies were the chief means of transport, carrying many types of merchandise, from tin to cloth, from the north of England to the capital. It took seven days to make the journey from Windermere to the

The Royal Bushkasi, Afghanistan
(Robert Harding Associates)

City of London. The leading pony wore a bell and was known as the bell-mare, whilst the pack train drover usually rode his pony at the rear. Sometimes, however, he would ride on ahead for his mug of ale and simply wait for the ponies to pass by the ale-house when, with his thirst satisfied, he would again join the rear of the train. Our illustration shows pack ponies still in use today, bringing down wool from the 10,000ft Lahaul plâteau, through the Kulu valley along the Beas river, India.

Only a few hundred years ago, larger horses were used for riding and small horses for agriculture. Then, when oxen were replaced by horses the need for larger, more powerful draught horses became apparent and one famous breed of horses, the Suffolk Punch—so-named for its 'punchy' conformation— evolved from an earlier strain of trotting cobs which were native to Suffolk and Norfolk.

A pair of horses can plough an acre of land in a day whilst three horses will plough two acres against the six to eight acres ploughed by a tractor. However, it also has to be taken into account that horses are vastly cheaper to buy, only a tenth to a sixteenth of the cost of a tractor. They are also much cheaper to work, require no unobtainable spare parts and can reproduce themselves. Finally, they subsist from the land they work and so do not need expensive imported fuel. I believe that if the economics of farming had been properly studied at the beginning of land mechanisation, horses would still be working in their natural element. They can carry out every type of land cultivation, including forestry, as these small tough Tarpan mares are doing in the great forest of Popielno in eastern Europe (see Plate 118). These mares are similar to the wild herd in Plate 1.

In the days of horse power on the farm, horses mowed the corn, carted the barley to the barns where it was stacked to be threshed during the winter. Then teams of four horses would cart it to the maltings and the breweries and finally to the local hostelry, be it the King's Head, the White Hart, the Horse and Groom or the British Oak. A fair number of horses were thus used in the transport of the pint of ale consumed over many decades.

Brewers' dray horses almost disappeared from the streets of our large cities but, before they were quite forgotten, there has been a revival in the use of heavy horses—the Suffolk Punch, Percheron, Clydesdale and Shire breeds—to draw the drays once more on British city streets. Provincial brewers have also reverted to horse transport as it is more economical and not so environmentally destructive as the diesel–powered lorry. It might not be a bad thing and even an economical improvement if horse barges were once more to be used instead of our roads being filled by 38-ton articulated vehicles.

Plate 111 shows a barge horse at work on the Oxford Canal at Brinklow, near Rugby—an old, very economical form of transport being overtaken by the faster, modern and more expensive *Royal Scot* of pre-war days. Barges relied on 'one-horse power', but by this means, many tons of grain, coal, sand etc, could be moved at a very low cost. The horses were of no particular breed but were generally of the cart or heavy horse type and were good walkers; plodding along the tow-path they covered up to fifteen miles daily. Mostly they walked alone and, at night, when taken out of harness, they were watered and fed with corn and often grazed the river or canal banks.

There are no jobs to which horses have been put and which they have refused to do, from pulling tram cars to shunting railway waggons. Launching or beaching a lifeboat in heavy seas was also no easy task for a team of light vanner horses. However, before the days of motorised lifeboats, when the men themselves rowed out to sea to save lives, the job had to be done all along the coasts of the British Isles by night and day, in high wind, hail and snow. The horses cheerfully played their part, but nonetheless, in the 1970s, the sight of a horse-drawn lifeboat even in a picture is very rare (see Plate 113).

The countless times that horses of all types and strains have stood patiently in wind, rain and sun, simply waiting, will never be known and a heavy horse's work varied between idleness and long hard hauls. The heavy horses in Plate 106 are wearing horse brasses, now much sought after by collectors. The idea of wearing some sort of amulet or charm may have originated in Egypt and it is certainly several thousand years old. The brasses were always made in specific shapes or symbols—a Shire I came across on a Fenland farm, for instance, wore a heart as an amulet, as a protection for its own physical heart and to ensure a long life. Certain brewer's dray horses wear symbols of the cock, perhaps because of a prevalence of old-time cock fighting in the particular locality where the brasses were cast, but the cock was also the symbol of vigilance and was used to decorate war horses, even being sacred to Mercury whom old horsemen admired.

The picture by José Luis Salinas would appear to show a horse and rider more on pleasure bent (see Plate 114), but herding cattle or sheep in the hot sun or blinding winds of the Salta, Argentina, is work of a most strenuous and tiring nature. The artist has here painted his ideal, when in reality the horses of the *gauchos* are neither clean nor particularly well done, and in addition receive very rough treatment from man and nature. When in Chile I saw six to ten of these *criollos* tied to a rail, and overhead, at no great distance, at least a dozen condor eagles were circling above and around a mountain cliff face.

The work of the cattle or ranch pony is no less exacting and a well trained cow pony is absolutely invaluable on all stock ranches. It is found in every country throughout the world, including, of course North and South America, South Africa and New Zealand. On the largest cattle ranch in the Kimberleys, Gogo Station covers 4,000 square miles of North West Australia, and here 8,000 head of cattle are produced annually. Were it not for the help given by horses, breeding and raising cattle on such a vast scale would be virtually impossible.

The Carlsberg Noriker horses are giving a different kind of help to mankind. These sturdy chestnut horses are descended from a strain of cobs which were native to the ancient Roman province of Noricum and throughout the ages, horses of this type have worked in many trades.

A similar though lighter vanner horse was used in all the major cities and towns of the British Isles. Called simply a 'vanner', hard, tough and capable of trotting on paved streets, its aspirations were humble. It lived to work and nothing else until the day when the vans, omnibuses and trams which it had pulled daily passed out of use as the number of people needing to be transported increased and as new inventions of mechanised transport came into use.

Appropriately this chapter closes with pictures of the Royal Canadian Mounted Police who celebrated their centenary last year when HM the Queen of England was presented with the horse, Centennial, which is still being trained in Canada. Meanwhile, the Queen takes the salute at the Trooping of the Colour on another RCMP horse, the mare, Burmese.

The Mounties and their horses, without which they could never have done their job, began their peace-keeping under the name of the North-West Mounted Police in 1873, and in 1874 275 men and horses made the long and difficult journey west from Fort Dufferin to the Rocky Mountains. The famous Musical Ride of the Royal Canadian Mounted Police was started around 1873 and features 32 horses, all of them black and standing between 15.3 and 17 hh. Horses and men have taken the Ride across the world. There are twelve movements, two of which are shown in the illustrations in Plates 120 and 121.

Many peoples, from simple tribes to great nations have used horses in wars, invasions and skirmishes to assert what they considered to be their rights. I know of no other unit of horses in the world's history, whose sole *raison d'être* for over a century has been to follow their motto, *Maintiens le Droit*, Maintain the Right. If all those horses which represent their countries abroad in sporting events were also seen as representatives on peaceful missions—as *maintaining the right* of ordinary folk to live at peace with their neighbours—what a happier world this would be.

96 Maltese cabby waiting for fares (HBP)

97 One horse's work is another man's pleasure (Bord Failte)

98 And the distances to travel are sometimes very great (Australian News and Information Bureau)

99 Freedom to stay, freedom to go but only if the horses co-operate (Hulton Picture Library)

100 *Crabfishers* by Heinz Düllberg

101 Horses belonging to the
National Coal Board (National
Coal Board)

102 These pit ponies were never asked in vain (National Coal Board)

103 Eighteenth Century Yorkshire wool traders with pack ponies

104 Pack ponies without bit or
bridle in the Kulu Valley, India
(Douglas Dickens FRPS)

105 'They also serve who only
stand and wait'—Highland pony,
Scotland

106 A pair of Suffolk Punches drawing a straight furrow—they are guided by the voice and listen attentively (Colin Fry)

107 Belgian carthorse, bells a-jingling

108 Dales pony

109 And Fell pony. In the north, these are the ponies that do all the work on the farm

110 Brewers' dray horses can still be seen on London's streets (Hulton Picture Library)

111 Barge horse on the Oxford Canal, Brincklow 1936, with the 'Royal Scot' thundering by (Hulton Picture Library)

134

112 *Flatford Mill* by J. Constable
(Tate Gallery)

113 Horses bringing in the
lifeboat (Royal National Lifeboat
Institution)

114 *Northern Gaucho* by José Luis Salinas (Tryon Gallery Ltd)

117 Noriker horses ready to
quench another kind of thirst
(Meteor)

118 Domesticated Tarpan mares
—these small ponies pull the
heaviest loads

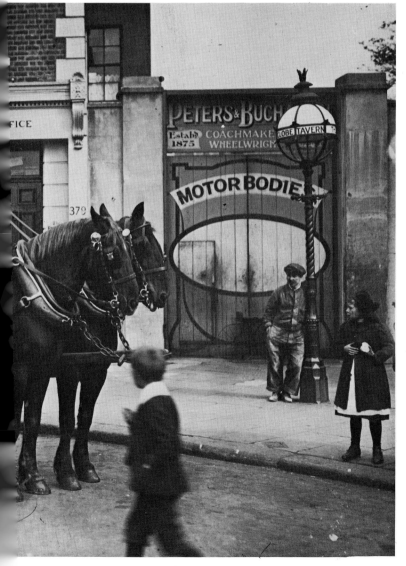

119 Until the population
increased, a pair of vanner
horses could cope with
omnibus passengers (Hulton
Picture Library)

120 The Royal Canadian
Mounted Police perform the
'bridal arch' during their famous
Musical Ride (Canadian
Government Travel Bureau)

121 And the 'star' (Canadian
Government Travel Bureau)

7 In War

Since the earliest times—at least 2000 BC—when man first bestrode a semi-wild steppe pony, the horse was marked as an instrument of aggression, as a means of increasing territory, or bringing revenge upon neighbouring tribes. It could be used to kill and lay waste. Yet the horse itself is perhaps one of the most peaceable and peace-loving animals ever to have evolved from prehistoric freedom to modern domesticity.

One cannot help but wonder if mankind is aware that in warfare it has prostituted one of the most wonderful assets of the human race. It has subjected a magnificent animal to the full gamut of degradation which is its lot during and in the aftermath of war. Of course, when man embarked upon wars, equipped with chariot-drawn or mounted units, he chose to see only the splendour of his heroic, beautiful horses and majestic array. He turned away from or ignored the result of his work, the dead and dying, as if the means justified the end.

On many occasions horses have defended their countries and the way of life of its citizens. There are innumerable accounts of horses rescuing their owners by carrying them out of battle although themselves mortally wounded. Horses have indeed helped to establish peace and have many, many times contributed selflessly towards progress throughout hundreds of decades and countless generations, until they were obliged to fade before the remorseless path of mechanisation.

Today, only a few countries traditionally retain cavalry units of which the British King's Troop Royal Horse Artillery is probably the most famous. The King's Troop horses take precedence over all other regiments. The last Horse Artillery Battery was mechanised in 1939, but the late King George VI expressed a wish that a Troop of Royal Horse Artillery, mounted and dressed in the traditional manner, should once again be seen taking part in the ceremonies of state. In 1947, the King wished it to be known as his Troop and HM Queen Elizabeth II decided that it should continue so to be known.

There are 111 horses stabled at St John's Wood, London. Most of these horses are bred in Ireland and most of them, too, arrive as four-year-olds to be broken-in. Their military training includes learning to jump and those with ability represent the Troop in Hunter Trials, Olympic Trials and Show Jumping Events. The most famous of these horses is undoubtedly Master Bernard who, under Sgt Jones, won a Gold Medal in the Olympic Games in Mexico, in 1968.

One of the official duties of the Troop is the firing of Royal Salutes in Hyde Park and for other ceremonial occasions such as Armistice Day and the Lord Mayor's Show. Like the Canadian Mounted Police, the King's Troop is famous for its spectacular Musical Ride with teams of six horses to a gun-carriage and eight teams in the arena together, executing the exciting and dangerous scissor movement at the gallop.

Troop horses of the Turkish Cavalry shown in Plate 125 are responding to a certain heavy-handedness from their riders. In spite of obvious pain, caused by the misuse of the bit, denoting an insecure seat, and shown by a resistance in the horses' mouths, these horses are still trying to co-operate and to obey the hand that guides them. This is a spectacular if unhappy picture of power misapplied. There are a number of State Studs that breed troop horses for the Turkish Army.

Upholding royal tradition in the preference for white or grey horses, Plate 126 shows George III mounted on the Hanoverian Cream stallion Adonis reviewing the troops. The foundation stud for breeding these royal Creams, was at Herrenhausen, near Hanover, and the stud was started by the Electress Sophie, as mentioned earlier. Unfortunately, owing to in-breeding to obtain pure white or cream horses, success was short-lived in Hanover, although at Windsor, the breeding of the Creams continued with more success for a considerably longer period.

The pride of place of the white horse is again brought out as the first Duke of Marlborough rides his white charger at the Battle of Oudenarde 1708 (see Plate 127). This was the third of his great battles, beginning with Blenheim and Ramillies and ending with Malplaquet. The Duke was a brilliant exponent of the use of cavalry, and his horses were without doubt descended or bred from the famous Spanish horses which had become so popular as sires at most of the European court studs. One can see this breeding both in the conformation and the action of the horses, whilst Adonis on the other hand, shows clearly his Arabian descent. (The minute detail in this picture by J. Wootton is worth examining under a magnifying glass.)

'Theirs not to reason why, theirs but to do or die' : and these horses too, could have died on the way to Mons or Ypres or any of those long terrible roads which led into and out of battle during World War I (see Plate 128). There is something grotesque and almost obscene in the carcass of a horse dead in harness. Perhaps this is because in life, a harness horse's trust in his whip is complete and he cannot know that he is being driven to death—that there will be no tomorrow. In this picture lies all the senselessness of war and all the heroism too of defending principles to the end since, senseless or not, loyalty to principles of right must be defended. These horses died defending ideals of which they were entirely ignorant. They served to the end and died heroically.

There is something both touching and charming in the picture of the grey gelding, Paul, and his companions (see Plate 129). Paul was the charger of the regimental doctor, during the German advance in the East 1940–44, and whenever his master lay down to grab a few moments sleep, Paul also took the weight off his feet and lay down to rest beside the doctor. How tired they are, these four good companions completely worn out in the name of obedience and duty.

Very few people in the western world know, in full, the terrible story of the flight to the West in 1944–45, of old people, women and children from the Baltic countries and the Province of East Prussia, before the advancing Soviet troops, as told in my book. The great German artist Heinz Düllberg has illustrated many impressive scenes which convey so well the atmosphere of that momentous flight and the part played by the horses.

His painting of the lonely horse gazing out into a dark night and an unknown future is entitled *Where to?* Many homeless animals were left alone and wandering in eastern Europe in 1945. Polish stud directors and others found and gathered up these well bred horses, some with bullet wounds and all nameless. Some were found as far away as the Don steppes where they had been taken as war booty, mares quite unused to the rigours of living out in Russian winter conditions and therefore in a shocking condition. But a visiting Polish stud inspector saw them by chance and later acquired eighteen mares for which he exchanged six young stallions. So the mares returned to their native East Prussia to be fed and cared for and eventually to breed foals, which later would take part in international sporting events.

122 The King's Troop, Royal Horse Artillery, St John's Wood (*Daily Telegraph*)

123 3rd Bengal Guards (Skinner's Horse) charging (National Army Museum)

124 3rd Dragoon Guards, India
(National Army Museum)

125 The Turkish Cavalry

126 *Adonis*, favourite hack of George III by Beechey (reproduced by gracious permission of HM the Queen)

127 *The Duke of Marlborough directing his troops—Battle of Oudenarde* (Rutland Gallery)

128 World War I 'Theirs not to reason why' (Imperial War Museum)

129 The grey gelding Paul with
his owner Dr Klaus Anstedt,
World War II in the summer of
1941 (W. Dietrich Kuehn)

8 Sickness and Death

The ratio of a horse's age compared to that of a human is roughly one to five. When we consider this carefully, it should come as a shock to realise that we expect far more of our two-year-old racehorses than we would of a ten-year-old child. It would be a great deal fairer to their physical strength and mental development if horses were first raced at three years, and, in the long run, a higher standard in racing capability would be obtained—the great Eclipse, for example, began his racing career at five years old.

Because of this forced maturity, Thoroughbred horses sometimes tend towards unsoundness, infertility and do not live to a very old age. Although, in passing, I have to add that I owned a grandson of Son-in-Law, bought as a three-year old, who died a natural death at twenty-three years of age, although his working life ended at 16.

Half-bred horses and native ponies, however, usually enjoy better health and longer lives. They are usually allowed time to mature, and consequently some are perfectly capable of a day's work at twenty or over and ponies can live to the ripe old age of thirty, especially those of the more primitive breeds.

The oldest horse ever known in Great Britain, was Old Billy who was stabled at Newmarket and lived to be eighty-three. It is said that when he was exercised down the High Street, the gentlemen raised their hats to him. There was apparently another horse of the same name, said to be a barge horse belonging to the Manchester-Irwell Navigation Co, which died at 62.

Possibly one of the contributory reasons for aging in horses is lack of dental attention. As horses become older, their teeth grow and develop ragged crowns, which affects the ability to chew and thus to digest food as well as making the mouth sore. Thus the full natural goodness of the food provided is wasted and the horse loses weight and health, so easily falling victim to illness or disease and consequently death.

The illnesses, diseases and accidents from which horses and ponies may suffer and eventually die are very similar to those suffered by humans. The difference is that, whilst human beings enjoy resting in bed, ie lying down, horses, for some reason, do not like to lie down when ill. Indeed, unless one is very careful, the very fact of recumbancy will contribute to a horse's death. Horses succumb very quickly to pneumonia and it requires very considerable effort from a sick horse, once down in the recumbant position, to rise up again. Yet if the patient is too ill to move, constant standing without exercise will cause additional stress such as swollen joints.

Owners are not always aware of the great damage which cold, and especially draughts and chills, can do to all ponies and horses. The dreadful practice of dowsing a hot sweating horse with cold water, which I have seen done during Olympic trials, can cause a sudden violent chill which may lead to pneumonia or laminitis, fever of the feet. In Victorian days, carriage horses frequently suffered from this affliction because they were kept waiting for hours out in the rain or snow.

Galloping, racing or jumping an unfit horse can result not only in damaged tendons and joints but in a severely damaged heart. Once a horse has 'broken down' it may require months of careful nursing and rest to get it right again—if ever.

Incorrect feeding will damage the lungs and, once this occurs, the animal can never recover to lead a full working life. The wind will also be affected if a horse is worked with a heavy cold or cough. Incorrect shoeing by an inexperienced farrier can damage the feet: 'No foot no horse' is a very true saying. And after a fall, however simple it may have appeared to the rider or spectator, a horse should be given time to recover properly.

Refusals are frequently part of the psychology of unfitness, pain or fear, and the *reasons* why a horse refuses should not be underestimated or ignored. A horse in robust health and properly schooled will rarely refuse to do what he is asked— even if the unwise demands of his rider result in a heavy fall or some form of overstrain. Bad eyesight, even blindness, is another reason which may cause a horse to refuse.

The photograph of Adana, an East Prussian, Trakehner mare, taken when she was thirty, shows an aging face, but the eye is still full of alert intelligence and she was always very much a part of her home stud (see Plate 134). As in humans, increasing grey or white hair on the face is a sign of age.

There is a too-common attitude towards a horse's expendability which is extraordinary considering that the British are supposed to be a horse-loving nation. Many horses and ponies might not only live longer but work longer if their owners had the means or the will to keep them alive. Whilst some owners go to great lengths to care, others shorten the lives of their horses through lack of attention and proper stable management. Yet, the British are not the worst culprits. Few other nations share the British soft spot for animals to the same degree, and for this reason, for many Europeans a horse can perfectly well end in a tin can or as a steak in a *boucherie de cheval*.

The only equine Homes of Rest of which I am aware, are those in Egypt and Britain which were founded by British women. Here, certainly, horses are cared for when their useful life is over. Often they are found and rescued from open markets in a condition which does little credit to their former owners.

However, to Britain's credit, she has a veterinary profession second to none and the techniques of treatment and operations have improved so greatly during the past thirty years that it seems a pity that so little publicity is given to this section of horse health (see Plates 131–3). The health and welfare of our equine friends is not subsidised by national finances but by private donations and normal fees and I venture to say that nowhere else in the world is expert veterinary advice so immediately available as in the UK. Forty years ago a Hobday operation was more primitive although just as effective as one carried out in today's modern conditions. A foal as ill as this one was at birth would have died, but this owner went to the trouble of having a special rug made for it and, when the photograph was taken, there was every hope that the foal would recover completely (see Plate 135).

I have seen photographs of foals with a leg in plaster whilst quite a number of racehorses have recovered from broken limbs. Of these, of course, the redoubtable Arkle owned by Anne, Duchess of Westminster, is perhaps the best known of them all. And there was also a Thoroughbred stallion in Brazil, which successfully carried out its stud duties for many years with the help of a wooden leg.

Medical treatment including the plating or pinning of bones, operations, and X-rays is available today at many veterinary practices and at the British Equine Research Centre at Newmarket. One particularly useful treatment for horses with injured tendons and joints is to make them swim in specially designed baths (see Plate 139).

To most owners, the death of a horse is an event which falls little short of tragedy, but there is also a certain sense of relief if the animal eventually dies naturally which, alas, few seem to do. If a horse has reached the stage when it is no longer happy, or has a terminal disease or accident, then it is preferable that it should be put down in the familiar surroundings of home.

Knackers' yards of today are well equipped and up-to-date, and quite possibly there is no opportunity for a horse to witness either by sight, sound or smell the death of another—even so an old pony, a favourite hunter or a faithful work or harness horse, should not have to go it alone in unfamiliar and impersonal surroundings at its last hour.

The picture of the dead Haiti horse (see Plate 140) is very interesting since the animal was shot several decades ago, in fact, before the last war, and its skin and skeleton are to be found in London's Natural History Museum at Kensington. The la Selle mountains lie between Haiti and the Dominican Republic and herds of nocturne horses, all red-roan in colour, are said to live up in the high forests. There has been speculation as to whether they are a palaeolithic species which escaped the decimation which befell many animals and all existing horses, possibly caused by rabies carried by bats in North and South America; or whether these horses are simply the remnants of those left behind by the conquistadors.

The memorial stone to Feiner Kerl is one of few, and I believe I am correct in saying that it marks his resting place (see Plates 141–2). This Hanoverian stallion, born in 1919, was one of the most potent sires ever to have been used in this breed. Stallions

156

of his worth are few and far between and even today in the 1970s people still talk of the powerful brown stallion. Feiner Kerl handed his outstanding qualities down to his sons and daughters, leaving 82 Premium stallions, 66 mares, who became the dams of Premium stallions and 278 mares entered in the Stud Book.

In many countries of the world there are beautiful statues to horses themselves or commemorating the part they have played in human civilisations.

In front of the University of Texas, there is the magnificent group of five Mustangs, sculpted by Alexander Phimister Proctor in 1948 and the words engraved on the base of the statue run as follows:

> These horses bore Spanish explorers across two continents. They brought to the Plains Indians the age of horse culture. Texas cowboys rode them to extend the ranching occupation clear to the plains of Alberta. Spanish horse, Texas cowpony and mustang were all one in those times when, as saying went, a man was no better than his horse and a man on foot was no man at all. Like the Longhorn, the mustang has been virtually bred out of existence. But mustang horses will always symbolize western frontiers, long trails of Longhorn herds, seas of pristine grass, and men riding in a free land.
>
> J. Frank Dobie

Many thousands of miles to the South, in the second southernmost town in the world, Punta Arenas, Chile, there is a statue to a sheep pony, a gaucho, his dog and his sheep. And here again, on the wild and windy Patagonian pampas, the horse was the means to a way of life and a living.

In Durban, South Africa, there is the famous Dick King Memorial, and it was here that it was said of horses generally by Jan van Riebeck: 'Horses are as necessary to us as bread'. Half-way round the world again, at Yugawara, Kanagawa-ken, Japan, one finds the Bato Kannon Horse Cemetry filled with the gravestones of horses long dead.

The Greek gravestone is a beautiful 6th century monument in honour of an Athenian warrior and shows him mounted on a well bred horse. It is of a period much earlier than the Persian Wars and the original is in the Barracco collection in Rome. The statue entitled *The Dying Hun and his Horse* is to be found in the Wandsbeck district of Hamburg. How many thousands of these invaders from the steppes of Asia never returned home will probably never be known, but this is the only one I know of which has been immortalised in stone.

All over Europe, the horse is represented in monuments to great leaders, events and even philosophical ideas. In the courtyard of the former Charlottenburg palace in Berlin, a horse is used as a memorial to the Grand Elector Frederick Wilhelm of Hanover. Perhaps there are fewer memorials to great horses themselves, apart from the well known Hyperion and Chamois-saire, the latter sculpted by John Skeaping, on the Exning road at that great centre of British horse racing, Newmarket. During their lifetime on the Turf, and at stud, these two great Thoroughbred racehorses represented not only their own outstanding personalities but the combined efforts of many people: owners, breeders, grooms, studhands, trainers, jockeys and many others. Without this combined effort between men and horses, the tradition of the Turf would never have assumed that position of importance throughout the world which it has enjoyed for many decades.

In six continents, millions of horses and ponies have lived and died in the service of ancient and modern peoples. For many centuries few have been wild and free and since they enjoyed an evolution some 60 million years older than man, they have more right to their freedom and they have a greater right to be handled properly than most of us allow.

A horse's petition

Tell me
I will serve you if I understand

Be clear
I am willing if not over-faced

Love me
All God's creatures need love

D.M.G.

131 The most modern veterinary treatment is available (Animal Health Trust)

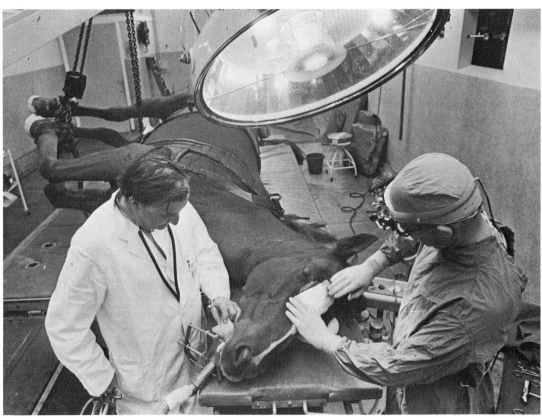

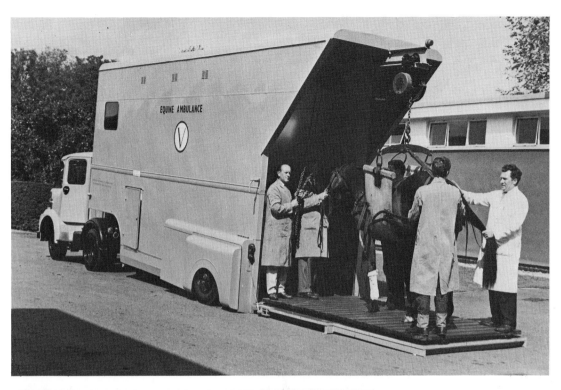

132 And the most up-to-date transport (Syndication International Ltd)

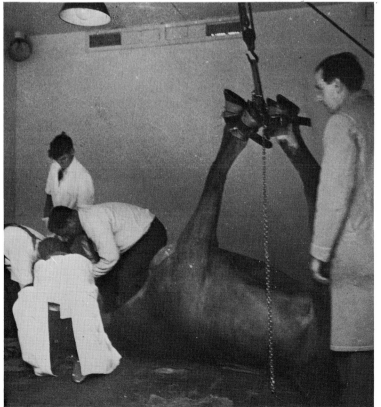

133 Forty years ago operations were more difficult

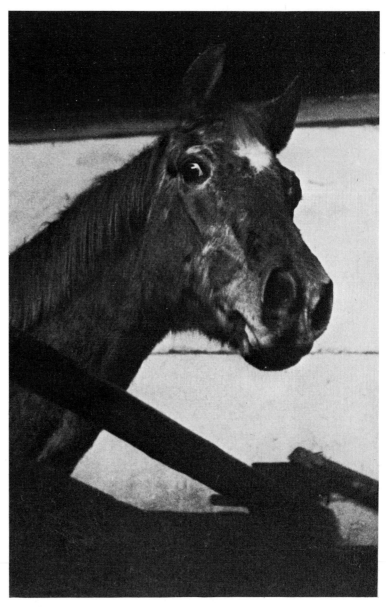

134 The face of Adana in her
3'lst year (Felızıtas Tank)

135 This foal was very sick when born

136 The face of a very sick cob

137 Ada Coles Memorial Stables,
Essex. Darkey used to pull a
corporation dust cart in
Gloucester (Atkins photos)

138 Bought at Barnet fair
(Atkins photos)

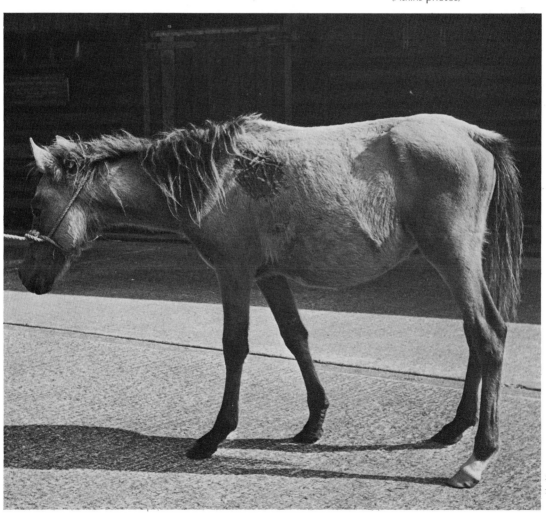

139 Swimming treatment for
horses recovering from leg
injuries (Syndication
International Ltd)

140 Wild horse, shot for the
B M. These Haiti wild horses are
found high in the mountains in
Haiti

141–2 Feiner Kerl: in life and death (Verband der hannoverscher Warmblutzüchter)

166

143 Greek grave statue (Attischen Grabreliefs Conze)

144 The dying Hun and his horse, Hamburg, Wandsbeck

145 Memorial to Hyperion

146 Charlottenburg, Berlin